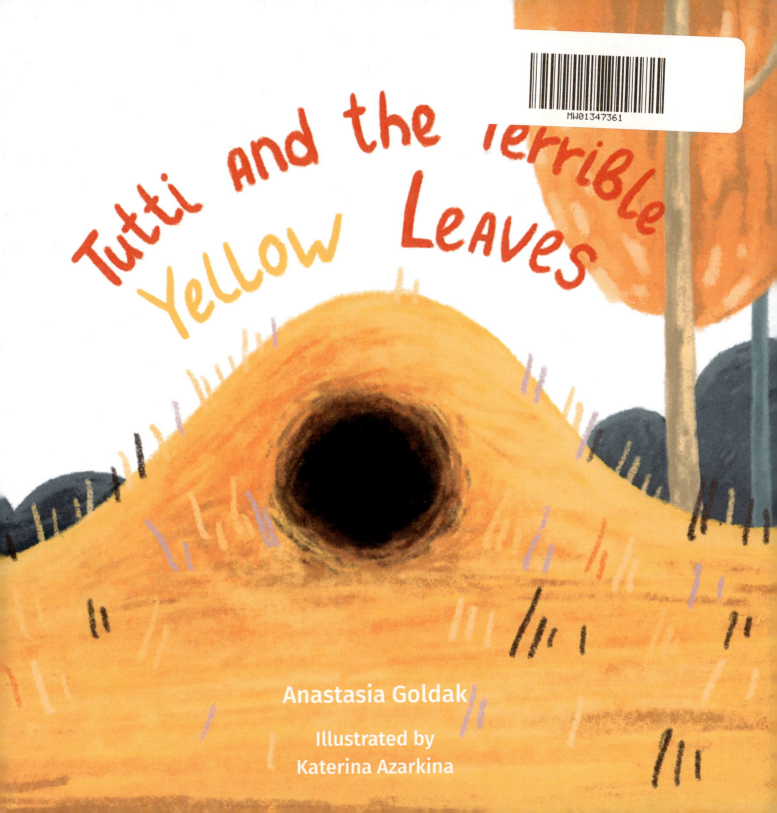

Tutti and the Terrible Yellow Leaves

Anastasia Goldak

Illustrated by
Katerina Azarkina

Once upon a time, all went totally wrong for Tutti the Racoon.
He woke up one morning in his forest and suddenly discovered that his favorite green trees had turned yellow. Tutti could not believe his eyes! He loved his forest so much. It used to be green all over, and green was his favorite color!

He wanted everything to go back to how it used to be: fresh and lush and green. He quickly ran up to the nearest tree and yelled, "Hey, you there! Give me back my favorite color!"

Tutti looked up the tree furiously, but nothing changed. Then the little racoon decided to ask nicely, "Dear leaves, could you please become the way you were before?"

But no matter how hard Tutti tried, the leaves stayed yellow.
Suddenly he spotted an unusual creature sitting in a nearby tree. It was an elderly forest elf, dressed in a cute costume with a funny hat.

"Let me introduce you to Frustration!" the elf said to Tutti.

"Fructation?" the racoon asked, confused.

"Nah, not fructation, it's Frus-tra-tion!" the elf repeated his word in parts.

"And what is that?" Tutti still was puzzled.

"Oh, it's an emotion, and one of the most important ones on Earth!"

This word was new to little Tutti the Racoon.

"It comes to us when something does not go the way we want it to," the elf explained.

"Oh yes! I totally didn't want the trees to turn yellow!" yelled Tutti. His eyebrows moved toward each other and his mouth squeezed into a thin line.

"Yes, I know, it often happens to me, too," replied the elf. "Today, for example, I wanted to munch on my favorite raspberries. But when I came to my raspberry bush, I saw that not a single berry was left on it. Oh, how angry I became!"

The elf then jumped to the ground, fists clenched, and started swinging them high in the air.

"I got angry too!" Tutti shouted. "I was running and yelling and demanding that everything turned green again. But so what? Nothing changed! Why do I need your silly frustration if it doesn't work at all?"

"It works a lot! Sometimes. Worked for me many times. It pushes us to try again and again, gives us more power, and very often helps us to change the things we don't like."

"But I also tried again and again," said Tutti the Racoon resentfully. He began to feel sad.

"Yes, that's the point. Some situations we cannot change, no matter how hard we try. When I realized that the bushes had no more raspberries, I wanted... to break them!" The elf cried out the last words in anguish.

"And sometimes I want to bite, kick, scratch, and throw things!" The elf acted out his words as he spoke.
"Me too! I also wanted to hit those trees!" Tutti squeezed his fists shut and swung at the closest tree.
He almost hit it, but then suddenly...

He recalled how he came here with his mom in the summertime, and they were sitting beneath this very tree. His mom took Tutti's favorite sandwiches out of the woven basket, and he remembered how yummy they were! These memories caused a pleasant warmth to spill over his body. He noticed that his fists were not squeezed as tightly, and his hands no longer wanted to hit the tree.

"Hitting and biting won't help anyway," said Tutti sadly. "That won't make trees green again."
"Yeah, kid, you are correct here."

"So, what should I do then? How can I make the trees become green again?" Tutti asked softly.

The elf watched Tutti with his sad eyes.
"Sometimes," he replied quietly, "we cannot change things. And at these times, the only thing we can do is—"
"Yes, what?" Tutti interrupted as his heart skipped a beat.
"Cry."
"What?!"
"Yeah, kid. Sometimes, tears are the best way out of a situation that we cannot change."
"Cry? But why? I don't like crying at all."
"I know, Tutti, but sometimes it's all that's left to do," the elf said sadly as he recalled his favorite berries.
"Oh raspberries, my dear raspberries." The elf's eyes shone brightly with tears.

Tutti let his eyes wander from one tree to another. Then it hit him: there is no way to reverse this; leaves will keep yellowing and falling. And all at once, he got very sad. Suddenly he realized that no matter how hard he argued, ordered, or asked, nothing would happen. And with that new understanding, he wept bitter, bitter tears.
Tutti cried. With every tear drop, his sadness became lighter and lighter. He felt as though tears were taking his anger out of his body. The elf stayed next to Tutti and quietly supported him. He was old and wise; he knew all about emotions, and therefore understood that when someone cried, nobody should interrupt tears with words.

And then, when all of Tutti's tears were out, he did not want to cry anymore. He felt surprisingly light inside, though still a bit sad. He felt that this sadness would stay with him for a while and would remind him of green leaves, of the time when he and his mom came to this place.
And it did not matter what color the leaves were, green or...

Suddenly, Tutti looked up the trees again, and noticed how very yellow they had become—and how beautiful! Leaves sparkled like gold in the autumn sun! Surprised, he noticed that they were all of different shades, some were yellow, some were orange, some were brown, some were burgundy, and others were bright red! How was it even possible? It was a real miracle! He started running around the trees, picking up fallen leaves, throwing them into the air and laughing as the colors showered down around him. He yelled out to the elf, "Look how beautiful this is!"

The elf looked at him with a smile and said, "And this, my dear, is a very different emotion." With those words the elf vanished behind the leaves, knowing very well that he would see little Tutti the Racoon on many more occasions.

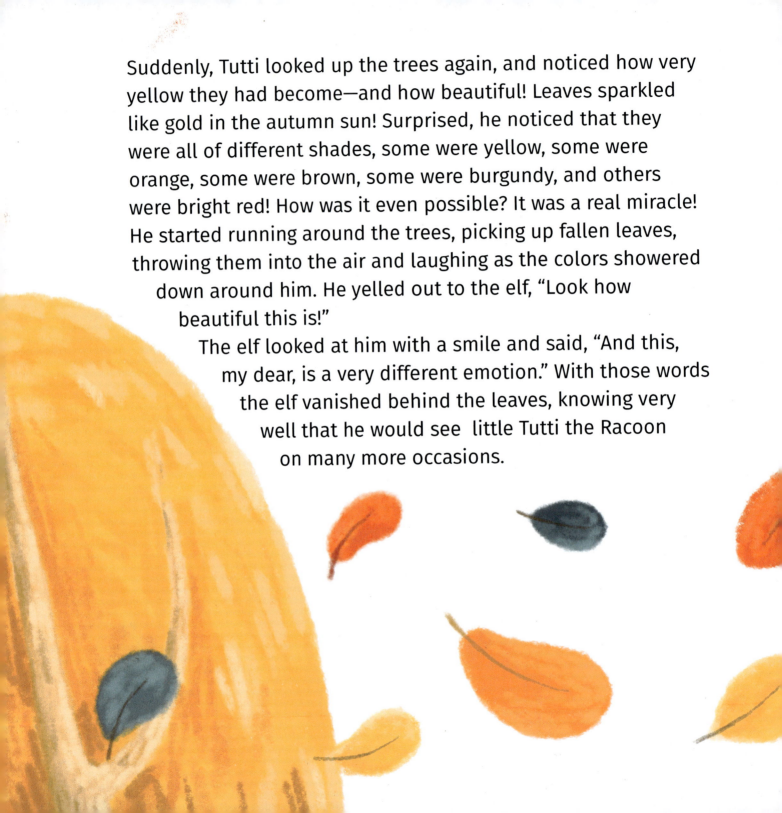

Inspired by Gordon Neufeld

Copyright © 2021 by Anastasia Goldak

All rights reserved. No part of this book may be reproduced or used in any manner without written permission of the copyright owner except for the use of quotations in a book review.
For information regarding permission, write to Anastasia Goldak: anastasiagoldak.author@gmail.com
ISBN 978-1-955733-04-5

Made in the USA
Monee, IL
20 December 2022

23220337R00021